KATIE WISMER

poems for
the end
of the
world

Ahimsa Press
Poems for the End of the World
Copyright © 2020 by Katie Wismer

Cover design: Christina Hitchmough
instagram.com/christinalouise.h

ISBN: 978-1-7346115-3-3

www.katiewismer.com

First Edition: October 2020

10 9 8 7 6 5 4 3 2 1

KATIE WISMER

poems for
the end
of the
world

Ahimsa Press

for my readers

also by Katie Wismer

The Sweetest Kind of Poison

The Anti-Virginity Pact

CONTENTS

I.
WAKING UP

he used to kiss my ankles
and I don't know why I liked that so much
now I drink wine almost every night
just to cope with being alive
I can't picture myself ten years from now
and worry that's some sort of premonition
I debate if making my art is worth it
if its fleeting impact is enough to matter
but I don't know how to do anything else
I don't know how to be anything else
I don't want anything else

I've drunk so much poison
I fear my lips are stained with it
that I don't know how to love
without digging in my nails
or bracing my muscles
and I don't understand
how people balance
protecting their hearts
with letting other people see them
and we're all so good at pretending
we don't care
that loneliness has become
an epidemic
my loneliness has become
an epidemic

they tell you to love yourself
before you let anyone else
so now here I stand
on this mountain
of confidence and achievements
I've spent my whole life building
and I look around wondering
if anyone will even know
how to find me
all the way
up here

I am a reflective compartment
for fake endorphins

an accidental cheerleader
for addiction

a love letter for the
desperate, exhausted
seducing promise

of brighter colors
and happier days

I am a collection
of the unwanted

everything you can bear to part with
everything you don't need
leave with me

until I am a pile
a heap
a load

weighed down
by the collective mass
and knowledge

that everything inside of me
is something someone else
didn't want

I am a therapist
a friend
a confidant

a knife to split open your veins
until the truth runs down your fingertips
and collects into some
semblance of understanding

I am your thoughts
a catalyst
a roadmap
a mode of transportation
to make the intangible so
very, very real

I am your greatest ally

at least
until I run out of ink

but above all
I am tired
of trying to be
anything else

I've lived inside of my head
for so long
sometimes I forget
there's an entire world
outside of it

the first man I loved
was not a man
and it wasn't love

and my first heartbreak
was not my heart
but I did break

and I bled quietly
until I understood
the difference

I'm just so thankful
I can now find poetry
in things other than ~~you~~ him

I no longer want him
but still
I hold onto his memory

somehow
every poem is about him
even the ones that are not

because before I met him
I was *her*
and now that he's gone
I am *me*

and most days
I am at peace with that

but sometimes
on late nights
in quiet moments
I wonder
if that is not a good thing

~~you are~~
he was

clogged arteries
festering wounds
and splintered bones

~~there is~~
there was nothing romantic
about toxicity

only regret
in letting the ugliness inside of ~~you~~ him
poison parts of me

~~I'm done trying to turn that pain~~
~~into something beautiful~~
I'm done trying to turn that pain
into something beautiful

when I met him
my life was so narrow
and limited

but since he left
I've opened so many doors
and found so many windows

now there's more space
than I ever could have imagined

and there are so many places
for the pain to go

so I guess
I don't have to hold onto it anymore

for a long time
I thought that
it would kill me

that I would
keep looking
for his face
in every man I saw

that once his
voice melted
between my ribs
my body would
never stop pulsing
with the sound
of him

and even if
I managed
to pull myself
out of the wreckage

I would never
be capable
of loving
that recklessly
again

I tried a few times
with a few other men

and it was fun
even though
it never lasted

but it took me
years
to realize

the only thing
that would save me
was finding comfort
in being alone again

it took me a long time to understand

that it doesn't take him putting
a knife to my throat
or a gun to my head
or binds to my wrists

for it to be wrong

sometimes
it's as simple
as saying

I don't want to

and him not taking
no for an answer

and through
the guilt-tripping
and the shaming
and the accusations

his manipulation
become the sharpest of blades

and somehow
I found myself

with tears
in the corners
of my eyes

laying there
and waiting

for it to be over

when he finally realized
I was the one that got away —
that used to be all I ever wanted
but I no longer felt
victorious or satisfied
at the thought of him missing me
as desperately
as I once missed him
I just agreed
that I had
in fact
gotten away

and I kept moving

I keep staring at blank pages
constantly reminding myself
to unclench my jaw
and asking myself

what do I want to write?
what do I have to say?
how have I changed?

a breakup can't be
the most interesting thing
about me

maybe if I cry enough
some poetry will come out again

love poems
about other people
seem to write themselves

poems about broken hearts
pour out whether
I want them to or not

but poems about myself
get stuck
lodged in the filter
of the different masks
I've worn throughout my life

and I wonder if
I will ever be able to unlearn
all of the hateful things
society has taught me
to think about myself

at least I've learned
to stop catering my life
to those who cannot
fathom experiences
outside of their own

I've spent too much time
agonizing over
if I am enough poetry
for people who don't
want poetry at all

here is what I know

anyone who tells a writer
they need a thicker skin
has it all wrong

my ability to experience
the world more intensely
is not a weakness

it is a building block
to my creativity
it is woven into
the very fibers of my DNA

how much longer
must we endure
a culture
that shames emotions

I'm starting to think
this world will just
never be compatible
with people like me

a slow stretch
first thing
in the morning

a shared laugh
finding common ground
with a stranger

catching the sunset
on my drive home
from work

the eager greetings
of my dogs
as I return

discovering a poem
when I'm not looking
for one

- moments where I find peace

II.
GROWING PAINS

gifted is
a classroom
for *special* children

who have
learned to see
average
as a dirty word

remarkable is
the achievements
and goals
and milestones
you're expected to have

so you can be
consistently growing
above those who are
ordinary

and I wonder
if I had been
average
all along

how I would've
turned out

would that version of me
be better

would she be free
of the crippling expectations

the internal need
to be better
and more

in order
to deserve
to be alive

would she be
more alive

I am not a windup toy
or an application for an award
I am not tireless
or only worthy
when I am succeeding

- *things to remember*

some days I feel like
a struggling metaphor

a lone descriptor without its pair

a moth searching for the moon
certain I've found the right direction
but I just keep hitting glass

a paper full of scratched out ideas
the perfect word just out of reach

a girl in a woman's body
just trying to remember how to breathe

it's easy to tell
when I'm uncomfortable

because
I become
a lot nicer
than I actually am

my cheeks ache
unaccustomed
to prolonged smiling

my soul burns
with the forever
unresolved need
for everyone
to like me

even if
I don't like them

my voice changes pitch
my hands cling
to rings
or necklaces
or clothing
trying to anchor themselves
to my body

and in my head
everything is calm
and logical

but sometimes
it feels like
the connecting wire
from my body
to my mind

short-circuits

and this anxiety
is a rolling wave
and I am lost
at sea

and I wonder
how many times
I can cheat fate
before it
pulls me
under

sometimes my heart
gets a little heavy

and I see the world in colors
other people can't see

so I bury myself
deep into my sheets

until I'm ready to get up
and my muscles won't fail me

it passes like the seasons
it changes like the leaves

it fills me up like smoke
that my lungs try to breathe

I wonder if you cut me open
how much soot would there be

or is that something else
only I'll ever see

is my brain
wired wrong

or is everyone else
as tortured
by the
glaring
awareness
of their
own
existence

do I
just pay
too much
attention

being in my 20s feels like
stumbling through life
wearing the wrong size shoes

always showing up to events
under or overdressed

mistaking lipstick for eyeshadow
and not being able to take it off

reaching the summit of a 14er
utterly exhausted and spent
sweat dripping down my nose
muscles quivering, begging for rest

and realizing

that was just one
of many climbs
to come

we carefully winged our eyeliner
and picked out our favorite jeans
just to down a bottle of wine each
and drown ourselves in a sea of people
who had done the same

and at the end of the night
after some of us had scattered to fall
into the arms of boys
whose faces we never saw

I'll never forget the look in her eyes
because she hadn't found
what she was hunting for

I wonder if she noticed
that all of ours looked the same

I spent
a lot of time
wondering
when I was
younger

how much better
my life would be
if I were
smaller

as if
I would
lose pieces
of myself
along with
the weight

and become
a different person
all together

and now
every day

as I pull on pants
that aren't
a size two

I think
of myself
at sixteen years old

and I wish
I could
tell her

that I'm

so much
happier now

than her
twelve hundred calories
ever made her

the jeans I wore in high school
don't fit me anymore
and neither do some of my dreams

- *it's okay to let those go too*

whenever I get scared
or the anxiety
gets to be so much

that it feels like
my skin is trying to
escape from my body

I look back at the girl
who lived alone
in a foreign country
for six months

so sick
she wasn't sure
she'd make it through
the night

I think of the girl
who went on
all of those first dates

even though
she was so nervous
she lost her appetite
for a week

I think of the girl
who decided
she no longer cared
what other people thought of her

and sat down
in front of a camera
in her bedroom

and I think

well
I certainly can't let her down

this home of flesh and blood
is trying its best
to keep me afloat
working overtime
to keep up
with the demands
of a healthy society

and I refuse to resent
or criticize it
the way everyone else does
when it's doing the best
it fucking can

I can't let myself wonder
how much more I could do with my life
or how much more I could be
if half of my days
weren't stolen by the sickness

if I didn't spend the days out of bed
drowning in a haze
of fatigue and weakness
if I had a body
that didn't have to fight so hard

because I refuse
to spend the time I do have
filled with resentment
and sorrow

feeling sorry for myself
won't make me healthy

some days
my body gives me
razor blades for teeth

the raw, exposed nerves
of a burn victim
inside of my bones

drunk goggles
on a sober afternoon

frostbite
on a summer day

and I have to laugh
because all I can think is
how lucky I am

that it's taught me to demand
others be as kind to me
as I have to be with myself

and how to appreciate
all of the tiny beautiful things
around me
amid the many shades of pain
that no one else
can understand

- *at least it gives me art*

healthy people
will never be able
to understand

and each day
I reteach myself
not to be angry
about it

as my excuses aged
they became weathered
and dull

so I buried them in the ground

weeping at their passing
at the sudden absence of floodgates
to my guilt and regrets

I revisit them
from time to time
but I go empty handed

because now it is clear to me
that growing bored of them
has been my greatest achievement

I've tried
to fill this void
with a lot of things

alcohol
to numb
the edges

caffeine
to pull me
through the days

boys
to distract me
from what's in my head

adventures
to try to find
some color

art
to bleed out
the pain

but when I stop
and breathe

and just let it be

when I stop trying
to resist it

when I reclaim it
as a reminder
that I am alive

when I accept
that without it

I wouldn't recognize
the good days

I realize
that I am not fine
but I am okay

sometimes I worry
that I've wasted all of my love
on the wrong people

on the boys
who didn't know how to be men

on the friends
who never bothered to stay

on the family
who only used that word when it was convenient

and I can't help but wonder
if love is a well
that you can run out of

a question that haunts me is

what would you like
to be remembered for

when I am
nothing
but bones
and dust

I wonder if
I will be
remembered
at all

and if that is important to me

do I care
if I am
remembered

let alone
if I'll have
any say
in the words
people choose

but I guess I hope
they'll remember
that I burst into tears
at the sight of injustice

and then
I tore my life
from the ground
and rebuilt it
from scratch
once I found a home

in my values

I hope they'll remember
my laugh
and how often
I liked to
use it

I hope they'll remember
my words
and the little pieces
of my soul
I wove
inside of them
like shards
of a mirror

in hopes that
others would see
themselves
reflected back

but above all
I hope
they'll think of me
and see the parts
they liked

and be inspired
to be a little kinder
a little more patient
a little more open-minded

than they were
yesterday

I wanted more for you
and more from you
my entire life

and you laugh
and shake your head
when I say
I don't want kids

but the impossibility of it—
there is no version of motherhood for me
that would bring anything but
dissatisfaction and resentment
one way or another

and sometimes people
don't change their minds

anyway

the world is bound to explode
any minute now
so maybe it's for the best

the world's greatest lie
is that we should strive to be happy
all the time

a full range of human emotions
at our disposal
and we want to limit ourselves
to a single one

there is beauty in our ability
to be surprised
to survive pain
to learn from sadness

what a tragedy it would be
to feel only joy

how empty we would be
to feel only happiness

everyone's favorite thing to say
after going through something hard is

you need to work on yourself
you need to love yourself
you need to find yourself

as if there's a simple
five step method
and once you're finished

that's it

you're ready
for the rest of your life

but it's an ongoing process
a give and take

a battle
that needs to be fought
more than once
to win

and sometimes
you move backwards

you hit a roadblock
that makes you think
all of that hard work
and progress
was for nothing

but it wasn't

the relationship
you have
with yourself

is the only one
that will withstand
your life

and it's okay
if you spend
that entire time

working on it

no one
is entitled to my voice
and it is not my job
to alleviate their discomfort
by breaking my silence

my entire life is
on the internet
and the air around me
is full of noise

and for better or worse

everyone thinks
because they see two percent of my day
they have some greater understanding of my life
and how my heart works

and since there's a screen between us
they think their sharp words
won't draw blood

or at least

their voices will blend in enough
with the rest of the static
that I won't be able
to pick out their faces

on the other hand
I have strangers
who think of me
as an inspiration

and they think
that what they see
is all there is to it

but behind the edited clips

they don't see
the cloak of depression
I can't shake some days

the way I love myself so fiercely
until a man who is no good
comes along

the way I meticulously count each penny
no matter how much is in the bank

or how I worry
that I've made
all the wrong choices

and I'm caught between
letting them see
the mess I really am

and letting them
believe the lie

because sometimes
I need to believe it too

I'm so tired of letting other people tell me how to be happy

III.
CRUSHING
REALITIES

there is fear
in the vastness
that exists outside
of my mind
in the galaxies
around me
in the space between
my lips and his

there is fear
in the memories
that resurface
from the depths
of the years I've repressed
in the versions of myself
I'm still trying to escape

and there is fear
in the days
that lie ahead
in the pain
I haven't yet felt
in the hope
I allow myself to dare

that maybe this time
things will be different

maybe this time
is the only time
I'm going to get

and even now
I must remind myself
do not shrink
do not quiet
do not twist and turn
and eclipse yourself
into a version of you
that is easier
for other people
to digest

usually
people don't bring casseroles
unless someone dies

as if this buttered offering
will somehow fill
the heavy void of absence

and usually
people don't use *cactus*
as a term of endearment

because most people don't see
the beauty in the way they survive
on so little
without complaint
as they wait
for their next drop of rain

but there was no funeral
and there was no body

yet there you were
on my doorstep
in a pretty white dress
clutching a glass dish
in those pretty white hands
and in the center sat
your bloody, beating heart

and with no hesitation or explanation
you handed me the dish
wished me well
and stuck around
to make sure I ate

patience is a desert cactus in the middle of a drought
patience is a casserole slowly browning in the oven

but you are not a cactus
and I am not a storm brewing on the horizon

and I don't know how many times I can ask you
to please stop praying for rain

I tried to wash the dish
I watched the blood circle the drain
but some of the stains just wouldn't budge

my family is an encyclopedia of illnesses
it feels like living in a minefield
spending your entire life
trying to learn how to look
a million directions at once
just waiting
for something to set off

I cried today
for the first time
in a long time
over a glass of wine
and my notebook

it started out
with poems of him
of the long-since faded
bruises on my skin
and my heart

but as the light
outside my window faded
and I poured
my third glass of Riesling
suddenly
I started to write about her

and I want to describe her in this poem
so that you can know her too
but I think I might start crying again

I want to talk about
the blue hat she wore on Easter
and all of the people
who said hi to her in the supermarket
of the excitement in her voice
every time she saw family
or the prayers she led
over thanksgiving

and I'm trying not to curse
because I know she wouldn't like it
but

f u c k

it's just so unfair
to lose someone
so perfectly good
while she's still here

and I guess sometimes
it takes three glasses of wine
in a quiet room
on a Friday night
to realize why your shoulders
have been so tense
the past four years

maybe this is why I've had so many headaches

how long do we have
before my mother
is too lost
to be scared anymore

how long do I have
until the pieces
start to go missing
for me too

my childhood home is full of
old Halloween costumes
handmade by my mother
the movies we watched on DVD
getting drunk for the first time
posters of boy bands
ripped from the pages of a magazine
ashes and paw prints
pressed into cement
photos from before the sickness
burned all of the memories
and

empty spaces

I'm always waiting
for a text back
a paycheck
a day off
some good news
better weather
a new idea

and as soon as it comes
the clock resets
and I start waiting
for something else

- *how much time have I wasted this way?*

no one understands
why I dread my birthday
why my shoulders tense
like I'm preparing to be struck

being the center of attention
on a day to celebrate me
is dictated by the ability
to have others around
to celebrate

and each year
it's a sting of a reminder
of all the people who aren't

it's a wait I don't want to endure
to see who arrives

I prefer how invisible
their indifference is
the rest of the year

I am
so very
very
tired

of people
who preach
their love
of life

while leaving
all of the ones
already here
to rot

they are up in arms
trying to make women
prisoners inside of their bodies

but don't blink an eye
at the children too afraid
to go to school
or a movie theater
because they may
never make it home

we are a country
so desensitized
we're out of our minds
and utterly
bled dry
of humanity

what is the point
of living
in a society
where medical care
is a luxury

not because
there's too much
demand
but because
there's too much
greed

what is the point
of a young man
tirelessly earning A's
to get a scholarship
and pull his family
out of poverty

just for him
to bleed out
at the hands
of a peer
in the halls where
he's supposed
to be safe

and what is the point
of a young woman
who is kind
to everyone
until one person
decides that means
he's entitled
to her body
without her consent

leaving her
mental health
irrevocably changed
but his sentence
is light
because
we need
to think
about
his future

what is the point what is the point what is the point what is the
point what is the point what is the point what is the point what
is the point what is the point what is the point what is the point
what is the point what is the point what is the point what is the
point what is the point what is the point what is the point what
is the point what is the point what is the point what is the point
what is the point what is the point what is the point what is the
point what is the point what is the point what is the point what
is the point what is the point what is the point what is the point
what is the point what is the point what is the point what is the
point what is the point what is the point what is the point what
is the point what is the point what is the point what is the point
what is the point what is the point what is the point what is the
point what is the point what is the point what is the point what
is the point what is the point what is the point what is the point
what is the point what is the point what is the point what is the
point what is the point what is the point what is the point what
is the point what is the point what is the point what is the point
what is the point what is the point what is the point what is the
point what is the point what is the point what is the point what
is the point what is the point what is the point what is the point
what is the point what is the point what is the point what is the
point what is the point what is the point what is the point what
is the point what is the point what is the point what is the point
what is the point what is the point what is the point what is the
point what is the point what is the point what is the point what
is the point what is the point what is the point what is the point
what is the point what is the point what is the point what is the
point what is the point what is the point what is the point what
is the point what is the point what is the point what is the point
what is the point what is the point what is the point what is the
point what is the point what is the point what is the point what
is the point what is the point what is the point what is the point
what is the point what is the point what is the point what is the
point what is the point what is the point what is the point what
is the point what is the point what is the point what is the point
what is the point what is the point what is the point what is the
point what is the point what is the point what is the point what

IV.
DISAPPOINTING
BEGINNINGS

maybe I'm not past
my addiction to danger
maybe I'm more afraid
of being bored
than being hurt
and maybe I'd rather leave this earth
having felt everything
this body is capable of feeling
instead of trying
to make it out unmarred

I met someone new

and we'd been seeing each other
for a few months

so I drove to his apartment
even though I can't parallel park

and I stayed late
even though it meant
not getting enough sleep
before work

after our first date
he texted me every day
and talked about
how much he wanted
to see me again

he was the first person
I'd bothered to see
more than once
since the breakup

the first person
who'd seemed worth
a few hours of my time
in almost a year

and I didn't know much about him

our conversations
were surface-level
full of little jokes and laughs

laying on the couch
with tangled legs
instead of asking

each other questions

and it was like
he was an outline

a coloring book
I could fill in later
when we were apart

but as time went on
he canceled plans
and took longer to respond
even when he started
the conversation

and I felt like I had no right
to be angry
that he wasn't trying harder
to spend time with me

but then I remembered
my anxiety about parking

and being tired the next day

how he'd never offered
to drive the twenty minutes
to come see me

and I realized
there is nothing wrong
with wanting to see
your efforts returned

and crazy is just a word
men created
to dismiss the way
their actions hurt other people

it took me awhile to realize
there was nothing special about him

I had just decided
I was ready to have someone again
and maybe he'd fit

all of this time
and I still haven't learned to see
without rose-tinted glasses

I didn't pick up the next time he called

I wanted to ask him
to try harder
because I wanted to love him
but more than anything
I didn't want
to have to ask

he was stop and go traffic on the highway
at two in the afternoon
the sprinkle of rain that comes out of nowhere
on a perfectly sunny day
the kind of birthday candles you can't blow out
no matter how hard you try
and I could never decide
if it was a miscommunication
or if he just liked mixed signals

am I just treading water with you?

I crave a love
that is simple
with a man
who does not mind
that I am not

I'm starting to think
my greatest strength
is my empathy

and my greatest weakness
is having too much empathy
for people who don't
have enough for me

he's not worth the dopamine
he's not worth the ache
society has brainwashed
us into thinking
our happily ever afters
have to end with a prince
but there are so many other things
things that are so much *more*
that our souls are craving
if only we'd pause
to listen

I am indecisive
about many things
in my life
but never
other people

if you are underwhelmed by me
please just let me go

every man I meet
I am convinced
could be the man of my dreams

we could be talking for a week
or a year

we could have everything in common
or nothing at all

and still
I view them all the same

and I refuse to be
the person
who loves someone
for what he can do for me
rather than the person himself

so maybe staying single
is the kindest thing I can do

- *on falling in love with possibilities*

sometimes I miss
the innocence
that comes with
never being burned

how I used to feel
before I realized
I should protect my heart
because not everyone
deserves to know me

how easily
I used to hold my breath
for these boys
before I realized
I'd be better off
trying to breathe
under water

sometimes I miss the old days
but I don't miss who I used to be

a fresh start sounds
so permanent

a singular
pivot point

bridging one half
of your life
to the next

but one of
the most
beautiful discoveries
I've made
in my life is

I can have
as many
as I want

ACKNOWLEDGEMENTS

This one is for the readers of *The Sweetest Kind of Poison*. Thank you for taking a chance on my first collection, and if you're reading this, sticking around for my second! Thank you for your beautiful pictures on Instagram, your thoughtful DMs, kind reviews, and enthusiasm. The greatest thing to come from that book was my relationship with all of you. Thank you for sharing your stories and telling me how much my words meant to you. I promise yours meant just as much to me. You made that experience so much more meaningful than I anticipated.

To my brilliant beta readers, your insight and enthusiasm made all the difference.

To my YouTube family, I'm not sure what I would do without you all. I am thankful for your support every single day. (And thank you for pestering me about making this collection. I needed it.)

And to all of my new readers, thank you so much for sitting down and sharing a bit of your time with me. I'm so grateful to have you here.

SIGN UP FOR MY AUTHOR NEWSLETTER

Sign up for Katie Wismer's newsletter to receive exclusive content and be the first to learn about new releases, book sales, events, and other news!

www.katiewismer.com

ABOUT THE AUTHOR

Katie Wismer is a die-hard pig lover, semi-obsessive gym rat, and longtime sucker for a well-written book. She studied creative writing and sociology at Roanoke College and now works as a freelance editor in Colorado with her cats Max and Dean.

Her first poetry collection The Sweetest Kind of Poison and her debut novel The Anti-Virginity Pact are available anywhere books are sold.

When she's not writing, reading, or wrangling the cats, you can find her on her YouTube channel Katesbookdate.

You can find her on Twitter, Instagram, and Goodreads @katesbookdate or at katiewismer.com. She also makes instructional videos on writing and publishing on Patreon.

Made in the USA
Monee, IL
28 December 2021

87380075R00069